CHARTREUSE

ALSO BY JESSE LEE KERCHEVAL

Dog Angel (poems)
World as Dictionary (poems)
Space (memoir)
Building Fiction (on writing)
The Museum of Happiness (novel)
The Dogeater (stories)

CHARTREUSE

A Chapbook

Jesse Lee Kercheval

Hollyridge Press
Venice, California

Hollyridge Press
P.O. Box 2872
Venice, California 90294
www.hollyridgepress.com

Cover and Book Design by Rio Smyth
Cover and Author Photos by Dan H. Fuller
Manufactured in the United States of America by Lightning Source

ISBN-13: 978-0-9752573-9-5
ISBN-10: 0-9752573-9-0

Grateful acknowledgment is made to the editors of the publications in which the following poems first appeared:

The Antioch Review: "My Summer Vacation"
The American Literary Review: "The Half-Life of Grief"; "Sleep"; "A Dream Set In Wheat"
Chelsea: "Down MacDougal Street"; "On Being Still Alive"; "Poem to Forget"; "On my white door frame, her name"; "we traveled far &"
The Crab Orchard Review: "The City Where—I'm Told—My Mother Was Young"
The Dalhousie Review (Canada): "Forgive Me"
The Denver Quarterly and *Stride* (United Kingdom): "Children of Paradise"
Hotel Amerika: "Mother"
The Malahat Review (Canada): "Life Considered as the Thirteen Locks of Le Canal St-Martin"
Margie The American Journal of Poetry: "I Want To Tell You"; "A House is Never Empty"
The New England Review: "Cabo De Gata, December
The Seneca Review and *Poetry London* (United Kingdom): "I'll Call This Death Chartreuse, Your Favorite Color"
The Southern Review: "Death: A Definition"
The Southern Review and *London Magazine* (United Kingdom): "*j'ai deux amours & one of them is paris*"

12 11 10 09 08 07 06 05   10 9 8 7 6 5 4 3 2 1

Contents

CHARTREUSE

THE CITY WHERE—*I'M TOLD*—
MY MOTHER WAS YOUNG

Long ago
the lens of a camera
uprooted
this city

from Sacré Coeur to the far suburbs,
pressed it between the heavy vellum of memory,
so to reach it is to cross a bridge
much longer, much steeper than the Pont Neuf.

In this paper Paris, my mother is a young girl
waiting for her lover by a stinking canal.
Or so I've been told by people who might
—or might not—lie to my face.

I pour over Atget's photographs,
each street, each boulevard, each arrondisement
falling under his care,
falling into his camera and out of this world.

But photographs are illusions, devoid
of both *pot au feu* and the garbage
the cook leaves—though Atget photographed
laundries as well as bordellos.

I imagine my mother leaving me a message
by way of Atget. I close my eyes
and think I hear laughter
and telephones ringing—*but I'm wrong.*

I walk over the bridge Atget made
with his stiff little pictures

and find myself in the Gare du Nord,
all steam, white and gray.

And my mother, *ma mere*—
is standing on the platform waiting.
She has always been waiting.
Unless—instead—she never did arrive.

Long ago
this city
uprooted

Triste, I imagine her saying, *so goddamn sad*.

CHILDREN OF PARADISE

Paris is an egg. It is *the* egg.
Wide or narrow, it is a ribbon
of pastry, of moonlight, of butter.
Paris is the light
gliding over our eyelids,
sneaking in even when we try
not to see. We know ourselves
through Paris & in this
Paris is as private
as blood & as public
as humiliation in high school. I broke a molar
on a piece of popcorn
watching *Les Enfants du Paradis*
in Paris, watching that luminous cloud Arletty
playing the heroine Garance.
Like the flower, she says
after giving her name. *What flower?* the audience
always murmurs. Me too—
& that's what I love—
the not knowing.
Just as no one in the Paris of the film
can truly know Garance.

But what with the cracked tooth,
watching this film about Paris
in Paris turned out
not to be the rush of paradise
I expected, but instead,
along with Baptise the mime,
I was in agony. Baptise
from his unconsummated love
for Garance. Me from my molar,
from the pain crashing through my nerves,

& for a moment I thought
ammonia & chlorine bleach
had come accidentally together
filling the whole theater
because I was crying,
because I couldn't breathe.

Then Paris
took me out of myself & into the souls
of the stars, filled me with great pity,
with a sense infinite space as poignant actuality,
as the light from the projector
shone over the heads of the audience.
But there is more, much more
to Paris than that. In Paris, life
runs away, is a runaway
at play & passion is everywhere.
Paris dangles all possibilities before us,
clanging as loud as bells. The mind sees
as through a glass—*Heaven.*
The heart sees—as through a moving curtain—
worlds beyond the bones
of everyday.

DEATH: A DEFINITION

To evaporate   into a rumor
To be without   fixed meaning...

December on the edge of sundown
standing by the water
elms toss   their last thin leaves

into the wind   as if that would stop it...
My hair whips my cheeks
urging me onto

the black
& broken lake
Now night falls—   its whiskers

the prickle of winter   that season
poets use
as a metaphor for sleep

& for death
Such a metaphor means   less than nothing
to me now   Already

I've walked too far
on such thin ice   Already
I've said too much...

Mother—
what dialect do you
speak now?

DOWN MacDOUGAL STREET

For no reason   we set fire
to the homemade signs that shouted from the lamp posts:
Lost Dog   Happy Home Available for Summer Sublet

No Ghosts Here.   I Lost 300 Lbs—Call this #
to Be Thin like Me
We never repaid kindness. Or loans of clothes or bedding.

We owned   not
the thinnest goddamn dime.   We moved our feet
that's what we did

and our moving   was what did it.
Our steps appearing as learned
as intricate   as dances   though the sequence

was entirely senseless. We could have faced   any
direction
since what moved us was   an ache to move.

We would not sit still. We would not.

We would not ossify.   Not for anything
or anybody.   No homes for us.   No shoes   even.
Instead we held our course

were calm within it.   We had
our own two   feet.   We had the asphalt warm
beneath them.   We had each other—pack of pups.

We didn't envy   even God.

J'AI DEUX AMOURS &
ONE OF THEM IS PARIS

in the mother country of my mother where I happened to be born, illuminated city east of everywhere I am, berth of all embarking, port of all return, street of truffles, bed of sharp remembered pain, on the banks, steep banks, of the river seine—o paris, enigmatic antidote—o glove thrown down which, *par bon chance,* climbs my hand again!

O paris, if I return to you, site of my commencement &— perhaps—my cessation too, if I stand beside the seine, shore of my conception, whose water smells, even to a sailor, like farmland ripe with *merde*—tell me, paris, will this day be a reunion, a homecoming or a coming to? paris, I am full of questions about my accidental birth. on this imaginary day, will you answer me at last? "Certainly, my pet," paris—or my long lost mother—says? *"regardez-vous!"*

so I do & see the sun slip behind the sugared dome of sacre coeur, put the prickly sweetness in my pocket to munch for *déjeuner,* then stoop to scrounge the trash as my mother was said to do & in the hush, I pick weeds to use as flowers. in the calm, I find sticks to build a fire. in paris, I do all this in paris, city I love as incurably, as irrevocably, as impossibly as I happen to love a man who looks as sad as you.

POEM TO FORGET

Let's forget everything the two of us
Let's unknow everything we think we know
Unlove everything we think we love the two of us
Yes because this world is the two of us dancing
to a tune played by our school orchestra
remember how that sounded? What a joke!
Now forget that cacophony too
What has passed between us is beyond memory
memory as useless as lost luggage
waiting to be claimed at the Hauptbanhoff
back in the days before terrorists and bombs
before all the trash cans disappeared
But that's not a concern any longer for us
since we are forgetting our history
We can still have the last laugh the two of us
if we forget the names of the kings and the presidents
Forget too the names of the rivers and mountain ranges
all of which existed before names
pinned them like dead insects to beautiful maps
They will still stand tall or run fast after the two of us
no longer know what to call them
call one that thing which is moving
call the other that which does not
What difference would it make?
Let's forget too the names of the little cars and the big trucks
and of a certain fancy German automobile
you once owned in a life before you became a poet
ie a woman famished for words
Now become an amnesiac with me friend
a woman emptied of all the easy ways of knowing
Listen to the wind wailing through what we used to call mountains
Listen to the rocks grinding in that water we used to call river
So like the cries of those we once loved

Forget! Forget! Give up their names
as we gave up their bodies
give up this pain
for which there was never a good name anyhow
Grief too damn short like a sneeze
and no gesundheit to cure it
Yes let's forget and keep on forgetting
Forget all we owned the two of us
Forget our unmade beds our silence the stars
Let's forget the sun
which has done us   in the end   so little service
Forget our teeth! Forget eternity!
Forget how we loved each other the two of us
I'll forget your mouth
if you'll forget mine

CABO DE GATA, DECEMBER

In vain, the waves come from
Africa to kiss your feet.
You draw them back
always in time.

You talk. I talk.
No one is listening.

I am choosing rocks
to take home
as gifts. I would cry
but this sea
has enough salt.

I find a rock shaped
like a heart but do not
choose it. Who would
I give it to but you?

You fill your pockets
with broken glass
worn by the sea
to green jewels.

So like you to find
emeralds where I find
cheap souvenirs.

I notice your nose
is dusted with sand
& when I brush it
you don't flinch.

Maybe we will go home together.
Maybe we will go on walking

like this side by side
even if we are not touching.

It is winter. I have never seen
a beach so empty.

I want to say—we could run,
but where would we hide?

MY SUMMER VACATION

—*after Wislawa Symborska*

My non-arrival at the lake cottage of your family

took place just as planned.

You'd been alerted by the phone call I never made.

Luckily you were able to not meet me when I did not arrive.

The cottage was full of people you loved—I wasn't one of them.

My absence joined the others for drinks on the rocks by the lake.

My not being there made the sunset especially vivid.

Several women consoled you for the loss you didn't feel.

And me?

My invisible feet took me down the beach, not feeling stones.

I stepped lightly onto the calm of the lake.

Was it my imagination, or did I not leave you

gaping on the shore behind me?

Or at any rate, behind me.

LIFE CONSIDERED AS THE 13 LOCKS OF *LE CANAL ST-MARTIN*

Lock 1.
Okay, maybe not all lives—
but mine, born squalling
in a hospital two blocks
from the iron mouth
of the canal, that meeting
of nature—*the Seine*—
& artifice—*the canal's first lock.*
That meeting of nature—
my mother's useless labor—
& science—*the surgeon's scalpel.*

Sectioned, the doctors said
of my mother & years later
of me as well,
as if we were grapefruit,
crated cargo moving,
lock by lock, through the canal
to the linen-draped
tables of Paris.

But we were not fruit—
mother & I—
we bled more like cattle,
like cows meeting their red fate
in the slaughterhouses of La Villette,
before descending the canal
as meat for the hungry
carnivores of Paris.

Lock 2.
Today, on this canal boat,
we are tourists
traveling the opposite direction,
Seine to La Villette,
in three slow hours, ascending
all thirteen locks—
the only people working
on this boat the sailor
who will steers us
through each lock, cast
the tie rope, gather the stamp
from the waiting
government official
& the tour guide,
his hands full
with a load of Polish grandmothers,
me—half-caste American—
& my two small, restless
children.

Ah, but *Le Canal St-Martin,*
is ready for us,
opening even for such a slight cargo,
though the Poles
& I—no longer young—
are meatier than the crew,
or than my children
raised on toast,
that dry American
invention.

Lock 3.
We leave the third lock
& enter the tunnel that is the canal
in its early stretches.

Haussman—that perfect
expression of his Emperor's will—
covered the canal,
stinking as it was with commerce,
smelling too clearly
of what made Paris
all her money, to build
yet another grand boulevard.

He put the work of the city—
& its working class—
out of sight beneath the sidewalks
of the bourgeoisie. But
Haussman, Kind Dictator
of the New Paris, built skylights,
barred portholes, to let air
& light into the tunnel
& hid them in the parks
of his new, above ground world.

Now green vines trail down
to meet us as we move
through the circles
of wavering sunlight
Haussman granted us.
Ghosts, my son Max says,
pointing at the reflections
cast upon the walls.
He is four & takes his theology
where he can find it.
Poor dead, Max says,
*they didn't want to leave
their Paris.*

In the gloom,
I see rats run along

the tunnel's narrow tow path,
their eyes as bright
as bits of sky in what seems
a day long darkness.
I imagine being born
as both this dark &
this uncertain.
Not to mention
sickness, the soft sibilance
of death.

Lock 4.
But we do emerge & pass beneath
the Swing Bridge
of the Barn of the Beautiful
which stands above the lock
of the same amazing name,
the lock that raises us—
load of three Americans
& forty Poles—one step closer
both to sea level
& to God. In the sun,
we blink at horse chestnuts
in bloom & at pedestrians
who line the bridge above us—
one per step—as if posing
for a group photograph,
as if they were a choir
assembling to welcome us
to life or, at least,
to their forgotten piece
of Paris.

Lock 5.
Yesterday, in the lobby
of the *Hôtel Batignolles,*

my daughter Magdalena
sat on the floor playing
dreidel with a girl from Brooklyn
who asked her
if she had visited *Le Mémorial
de la Dèportation,*
that splinter buried
in the tender tip
of the *Île de la Cité.*
I heard the girl speak
of the lights—numerous
beyond even a grown-up's
ability to count them—
that represent
the dead.

We had only climbed
the tower of Notre-Dame
& tried to count
the pigeons. *No,* Magdalena said,
setting loose the top.
*But we saw the house
where God lived
when he was only little—
before we went wrong
& we killed him
anyway.*

Locks 6 & 7.
We pass the *Hotel du Nord*
which was *"un film Marcel Carné"*
our guide informs us, starring
Arletty, famous one-named beauty,
who, when accused of having sex
with a German soldier,
replied—*My heart is French*

but my ass is international.
My son looks up
confused. To him an ass
is a wild horse from Africa
we visit at the zoo.

Sex is life, I learned from being
born in Paris &,
as every Parisian woman
knows, also a gamble
with both *petit mort*
& death. Not to mention
the time Arletty spent in prison
for her collaboration.
But Max
is an American
& I'm careful what he hears.

& we pass, too, *L'hôpital Saint-Louis,*
built to care
for the plague victims of Paris,
that has a museum
of six hundred plaster casts
of sexual organs deformed
by syphilis & gonorrhea.
One fact, thank God
for my young son's sake,
our guide does not
seem to know.

Locks 8 through 11.
Now, the locks begin to blur,
the slow swooshing rise
of water is how the years
flow by. The Polish
grandmothers begin to nod,

chin on cushioned chin,
until we reach
the Lock of the Dead—
which brings us all,
even the oldest, briskly
back to life. Our guide explains
this was the site

of the Gibbet of Montfaucon,
mont for mount—a site
so high all Paris could see
who was executed here,
hung from sixteen ropes
on two levels
so the hangman
could drop thirty-two
into the next world at one time.
Even in death, our guide says,
the aristocrats were up on top
& so had the better
view of Paris.
Imagine, he whispers,
The ravens pecking out the eyes
of the corpses left to hang
for weeks. In the foreground,
perhaps a pile of freshly
quartered pieces from the guilty executed
in the city center.

He smiles, waves
a hand. "Thinking
of having lunch?" he asks,
"Let me recommend
a restaurant."

Lock 12.
& really—

what do we eat
but death,
each death a way of living?

Lock 13.
We rise like a cork
inside the 13th lock
& sail at last out of *Le Canal St-Martin*—
If this trip was birth
then we are born.
If death, then where ever
the dead go, we have,
at last,
arrived there—

in the basin
at La Villette—our destination—
which was once both
the slaughterhouse
of Paris & the busiest port
in all of France. Now
it is abattoir
turned pleasure park.

In the distance, my daughter spots
a carousel, a slide
shaped like a dragon.
I take my children's hands in mine
& we disembark—
headed, as we humans
nearly always are,
toward paradise,
toward the promise
of a garden.

MOTHER

—after Robert Desnos

Call me *bitch*—
so like the dog and the mother of dog
the flow of milk under sheltering blankets
glimpsed at sunrise when the world is not watching
so like joy so like sadness
it is the sun lifting its bare breast above power lines and billboards
I call to me those lost on the sidewalks or the interstates
I call to old Fords young articulated buses
scraps of happiness like old memos and post-it notes drifting to
the floor in busy offices   white/yellow/blue/pink as baby blankets
I call jumbo jets and commuter planes
Goodyear blimps space shuttles sky divers
radio waves
microwaves
Let all send out my message!
I call the smoke of bacon cooking and the smoke of houses burning
the rings of smoke from powerplants that bring the electricity
a mother needs to raise a son
Help me find the son who is lost to me now
I call other mother's sons I call everyone's daughters
I call the living and the dead
I call doctors I call coroners
I call school teachers psychiatrists counselors policeman prison guards
I call the flesh that is my son
I call the one I love
I call the one I love
I call the one I love
the hot morning unfolds its bright arms and perches on my bed
as my son used to do
the power lines and the billboards bend to my wish
the former sing my message loudly the latter shout it
those lost on the roads are found in coming home to me

the old Fords are revived by my voice
the buses are sent humming new on their way
the scraps of memos on the ground and in the earth
snap to at the sound of my voice like semaphores like flags of truce
or surrender
the post-it notes are gathered and taken home by adorable sons
whom I do not adore
who come to me as my own son does not
obeying my voice, adoring
the radio waves that spring in my mouth
the microwaves that echo my lips
vacuum cleaners roar at my feet
air from heating vents if it is possible ruffles me
I get drunken kisses from the stove and the refrigerator
the dirt comes to die at my feet I do not need to find it
the stains in my carpet do not shake me but fade
completely at my command
the smoke of browning hamburger clothes me with its vapors
and the smoke of toast burning perfumes me
and the rings of florescent lights crown me
other people's sons and daughters so long hunted find refuge in me
their children listen to my voice
all children living and dead yield to me and salute me
the former coldly the latter warmly
the school teachers abandon their freshly mimeographed tests
and declare that I alone may command their work
the school crossing guards greet me
the college professors invoke the revolution
invoke my voice
invoke my name
the bus drivers are guided by my eyes
the librarians are dizzied listening to me
the principals leave for the desert
the school boards bless me
all flesh born of woman trembles when I call

but the son I love is not listening
but the son I love does not hear
but the son I love does not answer

not now not ever will he answer
the son I love
the son I love
the son I love

FORGIVE ME

I am having a bad night—
my legs are phosphorescent in the narrow dark,
my muscles grieve for sun.
Will that homely star we call Sol ever shine again? Darkness,
my mother said, is the habitat of souls—
weighed down, as they are, by the clay
God used to make the human body.
My mother had insomnia like me
& believed if you lay unsleeping in the darkness long enough
you might meet God face to face.
I believed her. But I have never seen Him.
Everyone thinks God wears long white robes,
my mother said, but I know different. He looks like Jesus
just a little rag across his middle
like that fellow Tarzan.
You can see what He's got between his legs,
that rag being so darn skimpy
& tell He is a real man—husband & father too.
Now I roll over in my own hard bed.
Now the clock is inching forward
the night crawling on all fours.
I hold my hand up in the dark—
starfish, sleepy spider.
In the end, my mother slept
for seven months
making up for lost time
getting all her beauty sleep
before she went to meet her God.
He is crazy about me, she told me
before she rode off in that ambulance,
I love Him too—
but don't you go & tell Him that I said so!
O Mom! May darkness swallow me before I do.

I swear on your white head
to obey for your prohibition—
like a spell in fairy tale we break only at our peril—
prick your finger on a spindle,
eat the poison apple
& risk falling into the dreamless sleep
that took away my mother.
In the end, each story is so simple.
First my mother is born to sleeplessness
then I am born awake
then my mother falls asleep & dies—
I see where this is headed &
I'm much too young to want to sleep forever
so I interrupt this story to sing out in the dark
One enchanted evening, I will see a stranger...
thinking all the while of God.
I try naming capitols,
counting any animal woollier than sheep.
But my palms itch & the electricity goes off—
or at least my clock stops moving
& the silence whirls inside me
until the room changes into white after endless hours of wearing black
& my arms emerge in day
& my eyes see the Lord of Light
they see the Glory & the Way
Nobody, Mother said, can travel
down these roads alone. *Nobody,* I hear her say

ON MY WHITE DOOR FRAME, HER NAME

On my white door frame, her name,
a date, *December 10, 2002,* a thin penciled line
marking her height, as if she were one of my children.
It is winter again, and the ice hums,
cracks, heals over again.
The geese have flown again.
Only she is missing from this round robin rhythm.
I see her hand on my door frame
and know it is dead. Even her name is dead,
just as that date is dead letter news.
Really dead, not sleeping like my overgrown lilac
rattling in the stiff wind off the lake.
At the park, I look for her. The light
hits the hill she climbed coughing,
deep in her throat. Soon the air will dampen,
warm slightly, then snow will fall.
How I tried to explain that to her—
life long Floridian—
how it must warm up to snow.
By the lake, a figure of a tall loping woman.—
her hand at her throat, holding
her coat against the wind, holding
on for dear life.

I'LL CALL THIS DEATH CHARTREUSE, HER FAVORITE COLOR

She fought. Stabbing tiny slivers of watermelon with one chopstick
long after her body had given up on all matter.
For this, I don't blame her.
She took first to wearing no underwear, then to wearing no clothes,
her body the bars on her window, her body the door swinging open.
She never paused between hours.
For this, I don't fault her.
She didn't know she was hurrying toward death
when she was hurrying so, her long strides swallowing kilometers
miles meters feet inches then not moving at all
She waited out her death in the jungle she'd planted, the jungle
paramedics hacked their way through the night we called them.
For this, I forgive her.
In the name of her avocados, I forgive her—
heavy fruit that fell on her tile roof like bowling balls
dropped from an airplane, like angels thrown out of Heaven,
like my heart—that scarred, that bruised.
Until nearly the end,
she wrestled the skinny Miami squirrels for every one of them—
squirrels that stirred only when she stirred.
The sound of her front door their signal to run.
Then cancer took her breath.
Then cancer closed her throat.
Then she stirred haplessly or not at all.
The squirrels, puzzled, watched the closed door, the yard full of avocados,
as they waited for her to race them to the finish like always.
The Finish—her heart buckled and bunched.
Her lungs, velvet, tore open.
For this, we wept—faulting her for all those Winstons and Camels.
The ashes of her body those ashes.
For this, in the end, we forgave her.
For this, in the end, we shut her green door behind us.
Her world a lush robe—far too heavy to wear.

THE HALF-LIFE OF GRIEF

I know now why they say grief *struck*—
like it was being thrown down
& stepped on   because it is.
Like being filled with a howling blue wind.

I guess I thought grief passed like a season long drought
or hard luck with hail.
Instead all night in your shrine in my memory
a terrible light shines

& there is such a wailing & gnashing of teeth.

My teeth.   Me wailing.   O God
I thought love was the meaning of heaven.
Now, it turns out,

death holds the only damn key.

Today I found a wasp's nest blown down—
dry as dust—
& all I could think about was you dying dying dying

as if death were the endless
house of paper rooms

I cradled in one hand.

A DREAM SET IN WHEAT

the fusillade starts soundlessly,

or nearly; a gun raised shoulder height, a rustle of wool like the
blind murmuring down a corridor, then the sharp slap of shot, the
soot of gunpowder drifting up into the flat nickel sky, down onto
the hard winter grain. The rifle a silhouette in the dusk, the muzzle
too bright to see, then not bright at all. The dog going forward to
inspect what has fallen, the dog wagging, retreating with the dead
bird held so tenderly in his mouth, not a feather is broken

& I think this: For her sake, I hope God carries his dead home that
gently. The red wheat darkens, the sun gets caught on the sharp
edge of the field, more red bleeding into this already red dream.
What can I say? Even in dreams, grief makes me quiet, careful and
quiet. She said it was not up to me to return God to the sky. *He
lives there*, she said, *whether you believe that or not. So*, I say to the
dog who looks up at me, *What do dogs think—is there a God?*

The smoke settles on the wheat.

The wheat settles in the field.

ON BEING STILL ALIVE

I know grief
is boundless

       but your vanishing—
           after agony, after fear—
      withdraws

before this battering of water by spiked blue wind
before this brawl from lake to sky

I feel this need to ululate
I feel this need to bow

             as the enigma that is life rains down

blunt
absolving
blows

WE TRAVELED FAR &

we were rash. the map's crease

turned out to hold deep canyons,

a long sad song of voyage.

the gazetteer, the dead end of the road.

                    O mothers, be consoled,

if existence were balanced on a knife point,

if our crossing were nothing but a burden,

then the map would not be folded,

then there would be no map.

A HOUSE IS NEVER EMPTY

The dog fur, sprouting potatoes, stale donuts on the counter—
are occupants
when I'm not here
when my dog is at the kennel
when my children are at school
when my husband is wherever husbands go
The house a wrapper we forgot to throw away
that unloved
that lovely
At any rate I imagine
the furniture—table, bed, sofa, vacuum cleaner—as leading secret lives
Surely they gossip, stretch, scratch each other's backs
when we are not around
when the dishes in the sink have dried
when the stove is cold and waiting
then my corroded pipes, may sing, may herald truth:
that God is in the freezer or God is that which nibbles at the mouse trap
The words on the refrigerator are from God. The heat that blows
unbidden from the furnace is His kind gift
By the broom's mother, by the dog's kibble the house swears—
it is easier for an appliance to enter heaven than a camel
Or a mother
busy as I am
I think this morning I may stay at home.
Send everyone off, wave goodbye
then go back to bed if not to sleep
I need to hear my house speak
I need to hear my rooms sing
I go soft thinking about the exaltation of recliners
the glory glory glory of the worn rugs that grace my floor
But how could I kiss the dish rack and not seem mad?
How could I kiss the screen door
left propped open all winter and be convincing

and sincere?
My house is as close to me as any love
but how could I kiss my humans after a day spent talking
to the shingles on my roof?
The house knows
the house forgives
the house takes us in
sinners and saints alike
no matter our muddy shoes
no matter our dirty hands
no matter we leave the lights on
leave the doors unlocked
let the paint peel in the back hall
do not sweep the steps
If I flew above humanity
what I would see below but
houses & more houses?
As if humans were turtles who shared shells
As if humans were birds huddled in square nests
I might see bats who have made loose siding their abode
I might see wasps papering their homes hanging from dry eaves
I might see barn swallows who have become city dwellers
dipping over & under phone lines
See asphalt, tile, wood, tin or copper roofs
I might see that divorce equivalent—a house up for sale or abandoned
Is anything more sad?
I think it is the houses that will save the world
I think it is the houses that are the mothers of mothers
If I could fill my heart with anything
it would be the warm stretch of open rooms
it would be my crowded closets
it would be my sticky kitchen floor
and then I would open the secret door
in my heart
and let the world move in—children, mice, dust mites, spiders
But is that possible

in a life so short with one of these three endings?
A. in which I die in this house with my children near my bed
B. in which I die far from this house which is my home
C. in which I die alone
Please God could it be in this house? Or some beloved other?
Please God not in a room identified by number. Here, let it be here—
in the end, let my house sink down and bear me with it to the ground

SLEEP

The sheep in the marsh sleep standing up
the frogs squatting
the fish do not close their eyes but sleep with eyes open as fish do
dreaming of God's perfect water
I sleep with my eyes open too
looking into this dream world which is my real world
eight hours a day

looking into a space
between a fallen-down wall & an overgrown willow
where cement & grass prick
the soles of my feet

If hawks fly over this marsh
than wall or no wall   they can see me
as they see all living things when they're hungry
& I pray
in this dream I am too large
for something with claws to catch, kill & eat

But then we all have our fears—
the grass is afraid of the sheep
the dirt afraid of the rain that might wash it to sea
& yet we still sleep
Lord of the dream sea
Lord of this dream earth
the still night you ordered has, at last, come to pass

I WANT TO TELL YOU

I heard Joyce Carol Oates say writing
was like pushing a pea   across a warehouse with your nose
you crawl crawl crawl along
& when you look up—
dirty floorboards as far as you can see stretching   to forever.
I think she was talking about a novel.
I think she was talking about *Blonde*
a novel she was writing about Marilyn Monroe.
I am talking about this poem.
Pea & no princess, nose in the dirt
pushing pushing pushing & so little progress.
I am talking about poetry.
I am talking about breaking out of the neat little box of humorous lines
rising to a   *zing*
of cosmic meaning at the end.
I know—I've written them too.   Still do—
poems too damn much like Methodist sermons.
First the joke about little Johnny & God
(Johnny thinks the hymn "Bringing the Sheaves"
is "Bringing in The Sheets!"—
I always thought it was "Bringing in the Sheep"—
Oh well guess I'm damned).
Then the metaphor about how the minister's windshield wipers
not working in a terrible rain storm
is like trying to fathom
The Will of God
(in both cases you have no idea where you are going).
A quick reference to scripture   & pass the plate.
What about everything this sermon/ my poem has left unsaid?
About how we are dying all dying
how people I love are already dead?
this year   my sister-in-law
sixteen years ago in April   my mom

eighteen years Tuesday   my dad
in a day or a decade   me   & you too
don't kid yourself
My daughter told me she doesn't want to die   or get married
Some days I know just what she means
Now in the other room I hear her singing
LoveLoveLoveLoveLove   Makes the World Go Round
My daughter who turned 12 last night—*New Year's Eve*—-
& we all stood on the frozen grass of the Capitol square
watching fireworks   explode off   the glass bank across
     the street
Glad that's not our bank my husband said
when he saw the fireman poised   hoses at the ready
Hey just like 'Nam he added as a joke though he would know
Each concussion   a fist   in the chest
Each burst red/green/gold sizzling twisting
stars falling out of the universe & into our eyes
I start to laugh & I start to cry
& even   at the end of this poem
I have no earthly idea why